Victor Peters

FINANCIAL SUCCESS TOOLKIT

Copyright Information

Financial Success Toolkit
© Royal Seeds International, May 2014
Revised February 2015
http://royalseedsinternational.blogspot.com/

Comments and order details should be directed to:
victorious_gem@yahoo.com

Table of Content

Preface

This book is a piece of writing on financial success designed to assist you in building a strong financial future through tested principles and uncommon practices of many years of personal development effort. It explains in detail, the fundamental steps to financial success and how you can use it to your advantage.

If a man change the way he thinks, and apply himself to the course of positive actions and opportunities available to him; he will be surprise at the rapid transformation the effect of the change will bring to him; more often than not, in the comfort and material things of life. We often imaging that thought can be kept secret, but it cannot; rather it rapidly crystallizes into habits, and habits solidify into circumstances. Thoughts of fear, financial insecurity, doubt, and indecision crystallizes into weak, unmanly, and indecisive habits which solidify into circumstances of failure. On the other hand, a positive and determinate thought of all kinds crystallizes into habits of grace, temperance, courage, self determination and self control. The results of such thought is success, plenty, and freedom of all kind – including financial freedom!

You present circumstance is not a determinant of your tomorrow. But what you do with the opportunities that come your way today, determines the gains you receive tomorrow. Change the way you think; have the entrepreneur mentality. Don't confess success and always think poverty. The thought you allow in your mind is what germinates into character you exhibit; and the character you continually exhibit becomes your lifestyle. If you have not performed well in your finances in the past, at least be thankful that you have access to this financial toolkit. It will definitely make a huge impact on your destiny.

Welcome to your season of positive progressive change for financial empowerment!

Victor Peters – PhD

Financial Success – What You Must Know

Only by much searching and mining are gold and diamonds obtained and man can find every truth connected with the quality of life he lives; if he is willing to dig deep into the mine of his soul. This means that he is the maker of his character, the molder of his life, and the builder of his destiny. He may choose to watch his life slip away in abject poverty, or control it; grab opportunities that come his way and therefore change the course of events to his advantage and survival through molding a new destiny for himself.

Financial Success Not an Asset of the Privileged

Financial success is not an asset of the privileged, neither is it the reward of the fortunate few; financial success is the possession of individuals who are willing to follow the basic principles to financial freedom. These principles do not align with race, color, continent or even family line; it is a natural principle that will produce for anyone who practices it. If applied as discussed in this book, the result of success is as sure as adding 1+1 to get 2. Take a look at some financially successful people around you, and you will see these principles readily at work in their lives.

Financial success is a level you get to in life that put you in command and control when it comes to monetary affairs. Money is a spirit that has wings and do fly; how caring and friendly you are to it determines how long it stays in your hands. If you can handle a few amount with care, it beckon on others to come. '*See I have found a new home where I am well taken care of, friends come let us abide here*'. Suddenly, you see yourself grow in wealth. Many people think there is some shortcut that will help them achieve financial success. We all want easy answers without having to work at it or make any changes. My experience confirmed that this is not how it works. You do have to make changes and take some consistent positive action to achieve any goal in life. Even when things are dropped on your lap, like winning a lottery; on a long term it rarely solves the financial problem you have.

This is because the behavioral pattern over the long term will eventually take you back to the same situation again and again. Only few get out of financial incarceration through circumstantial reaches. I have seen an individual who won a lottery of two million pounds, but today he is back to the circle of the poor; begging for what to eat.

The question I'll like to ask you is "*how diligent are you in achieving your goal of financial success in life?*" The platform to launch yourself into your financial success may be set before you, but achieving your dream is your personal input. I belief every step we take in life is either with our being conscious or unconscious of its final end. Men are anxious to improve their circumstances, but are unwilling to improve themselves, they therefore remain bound. If you and I do not shrink from self-crucifixion we can never fail to accomplish the goals of financial success we have set for ourselves. This means that a man who is determined to acquire wealth must be prepared to make great personal sacrifices before he can accomplish his desires; and how much more is he who would realize a strong and vibrant objective of life – FINANCIAL SUCCESS? Our creator will always provide us with the opportunities, but grabbing the opportunity that comes your way is your own decision. You can increase your resistance to physical stress by strengthening your physical health; just the same way you can increase your resistance to financial stress by strengthening your financial comfort.

Financial Success Requires Physical and Mental Exertion

Just like any goal in life, getting your finances stabilize and becoming financially successful requires the development of good financial

7

habits. I've been researching on this topic extensively in the last few months in my quest to eliminate debt, increase my savings and increase financial security for my family. Being financially successful means you are in control of your money instead of it controlling you. Your income doesn't necessarily determine how financially successful you are – your choices and priorities do. If you are struggling, financial success may seem like a distant dream, but by following some basic steps, you can make that dream a reality.

Successful financial management is an ongoing process. It is important to continually monitor your spending, savings, and investments and adjust your plan as necessary. Fortunately, you don't have to be an expert in personal finance to achieve success, but a solid understanding of the basics can put you in control of your money. As an individual I have taken deep thoughts about life, and I discovered that we are the masterminds of all that happens to us in our journey through life. According to a popular author, "*the divinity that shapes our ends is in us*". To achieve financial success we must take positive, deliberate and rightful steps in the direction of those things that favors our resolves to achieve that success.

Good thoughts and actions can never produce bad results; likewise, band thoughts and actions can never produce good results. A man only begin to discover himself when he ceases to be careless about the issues concerning his life, rather commences to search for the hidden justice which regulates his life. When the truth is found, and he adapts his mind to that regulating factor, he ceases to accuse others as the cause of his poor condition; instead he builds himself up in strong and definite goals of life, kick against negative circumstances, and begin to use them as aids to his rapid progress, and as a means of discovering the hidden powers and possibilities that nature has brought his way.

In this Book, I have discussed a number of steps which you can follow to achieve financial success. It is termed *'**Financial Success Tool Kit***, a member of my launch-pad series. Many people think there is some magic bullet or "clandestine" information that will help them achieve financial independence with the blink of the eyes. We all want easy answers to our monetary problems without having to work at it or make any serious commitment. My previous knowledge confirms that you must put in something to get others. Nowhere in the whole world where you don't sow a seed, keep watering it and tilling the ground before the yield comes. It is a natural principle that cannot be changed. You do have to make changes and take some consistent positive action to achieve any goal in life. Even when you stumble on accidental reaches, like winning a raffle draw, it rarely solves your whole monetary problems all at once. This is because there is a pattern of behavior in man that always repeats itself over a sequence.

Money is a Mobile Agent

You don't have to know everything about financial forecasting or investment planning to be financially successful; but you need enough education on how to handle money, and cage it so it can keep reproducing itself in your hands. Money has wings and therefore can fly. It takes person with smart ideas to lock in on it and prevent it from escaping. And once you can successful prevent it from escaping; it beckons on its colleagues to come; and by this invitation, wealth the conglomerate of money will make your abode its final resting place. Friends, I assure you if you can successfully keep a thousand dollars over a period of three months without spending it, shortly you will be able to keep tens of it; and if it can stay in your hands for another three months, you will be able to keep hundreds; and the more financially stable you'll become. Just like any other goal in life, getting your monetary economics in proper shape will make you financially stable and thus open the door of financial success to you.

To succeed financially implies you are in control of your money rather than your money controlling you. What you earn as income do not automatically determine how financially successful you can be – but the choices you make and priorities do. If you are under stress financially, financial success may look like a distant dream. This is not true; any goal towards your financial success can be achieved if you set yourself from the beginning to accomplish your goals. Achieving such goals requires the development of good financial habits. These habits shall be discussed in detail later on in this book.

Self-Control Pivotal to Financial Success

Self-control is the ability to control oneself; in particular your emotions and desires at all times, especially in difficult situations. Put in another word, self-control is the ability to control the actions you take in your daily life and the decisions you make in a way to sacrifice for some other important goals in your life.

Self-control is an essential skill for proper financial management. Outside of it, monetary gains will be pretty difficult to acquire or accumulate in life. Self-control is being able to say no when you need to and to be able to put money away instead of spending it frivolously on less important things. It is being able to do the things you don't want to do when you know you must. It is forcing yourself to do the things that are necessary in both your financial life and your non-financial life. It is obvious that your wants will always expend whatever income you get your hands on. This implies controlling your spending is a necessity to achieving financial independence. If you do not have normal amount of discipline you will have to get it the hard way. Acquiring it comes from learning to practice it in small amounts. Start by simply trying to follow your budget. Once you can do this then the next step is to be able to save money.

A person with self-control for instance, is able to overcome spending temptations and distractions calmly and doggedly. Without that feeling of self-control, you end up feeling you have been robbed, powerless, and weak; but the truth is you can live without those overgenerous spending. Start small by challenging yourself to control your financial behavior e.g. cutting your spending for a short period of time, and steadily you continue to build on it. Many studies have found that people perform relatively poorly when it comes to self-control. This virtue is not common among people. However, you can train yourself gradually by taking specific steps to accomplish it. Later in this book a lot has been discussed about self-discipline that can help you take the required steps in achieving financial success.

If you are struggling with your finances I recommend that you try the steps discussed in this book and see what happens. You need to find actions that work for you so keep trying things until you find an action that meets your specific circumstance. Also, do what you can now; don't keep procrastinating with what you'll learn in this book. There is never going to be a better time than now. Keep working it until it works out for you. There is no harm in trying; not to try at all is worse.

Getting Started and Goal Setting

Getting Started

Friends and colleagues I'll like to ask you one question: what do you really want in life or what is your goal in life? Bad circumstances exist, we know. But the best we can give to any bad circumstance of life is to ensure we overcome it. Poverty is one of such bad circumstance of life that is prevalent in most part of the world, and so requires deliberate effort to overcome it. What does it mean to fight bad circumstances? It means as human beings we continually revolt against the negativity of our lives that tends to limit our happiness and social equilibrium with others. As an individual I have taken deep thoughts about life, and I discovered that we are the architects of all that happens to us in our journey through life.

On a personal ground everyone desires success, and no one ever wants to see poverty around him. But even though we desire success, that desire must be matched with will-powered actions for us to see what we really want. Financial success is one of those goals. The goal of attaining financial success in life must be followed by our diligence on what will bring that success to us.

In all human affairs there are efforts, and there are results, and the strength of the effort is the measure of the results. Power, material, intellectual capability, and spiritual possessions are the fruits of efforts; they are steps taken, thoughts completed, or vision realized. However, the thoughtless, the ignorant, and the indolent, seeing only the apparent effects of things and not the things themselves, talk of luck, fortune, and chance. Yes chance! It will always come to you at your own time. Seeing a man grow rich, they say "How lucky he is?" another will say "How highly favored he is?" One thing I have come to understand about life is that time and chance keep resurfacing themselves to mankind because nature will always work on our mind's thinking and belief to take us to the next phase of life orchestrated by that thinking and belief we allowed in our mind.

Repeat aloud the word "success" several times, and notice how you feel. Depending on your mental and emotional makeup, and your mood of the moment, there are two possibilities of what you can experience. You might become inspired, happy and elated; or despondent, unhappy and bitter. In the latter case, you might start telling yourself how miserable you are, and that financial success is not for you. This may sound strange, but thoughts about success can evoke negative feelings. People who have entertained negative thoughts and feelings most of their lives, expect failure and do not feel worthy of success. If they have experienced lack and hardships, they believe that financial success is not for them. In these cases, everything associated with financial success might evoke negative feelings. Your thoughts and feelings can draw or repel financial success. They shape your beliefs and expectations generally about success or failure.

Thoughts come and go and change direction like the wind. They influence your mind the same way that the wind affects the direction of a flag. One moment the flag may be fluttering this way, and a moment later in a different direction. One moment you might be thinking one thing or see things from a certain viewpoint, and a moment later this can change.

When your thoughts, feelings and moods become steady and under your control, your life also comes under your control. You become the deciding factor, not the outside influences or passing moods. In order to control your thoughts, feelings and moods which are essential tools to navigate your life; concentration and willpower need to be developed. Concentration and willpower constitute the steering wheel of your life, with which you can navigate the boat of your life toward success and achievement.

Goal Setting and Tracking

Identifying and setting clear, achievable goals is a crucial part of anyone's financial growth plan. A financial success goal is the exact time-dependent schedule of what is to be achieved over a period of time.

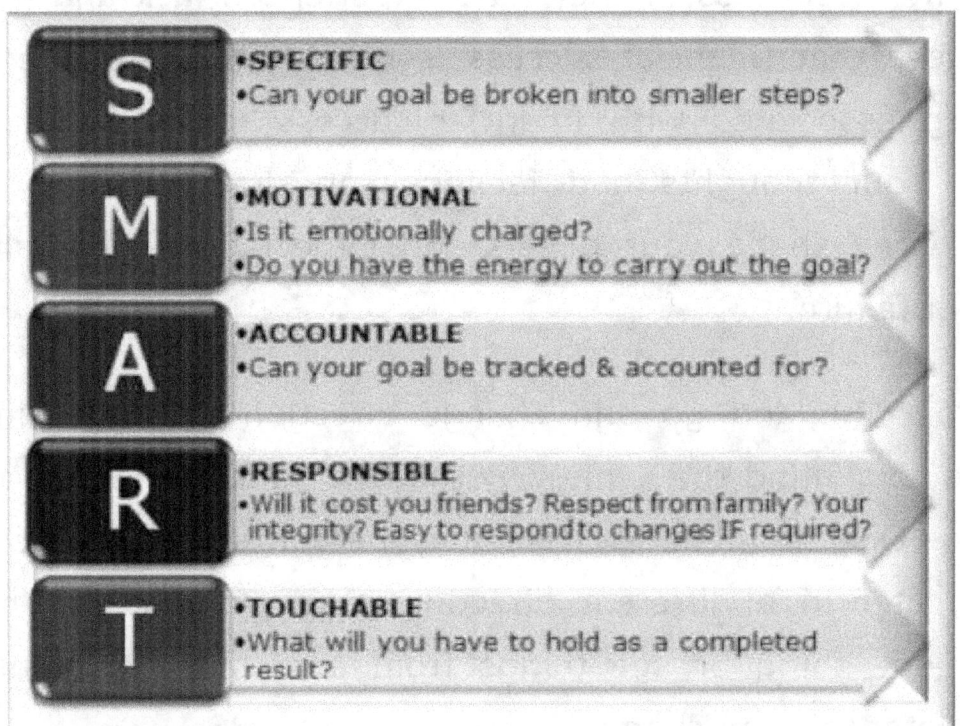

For instance, in the next five years I plan to take my business to a level of total asset amounting to US$10 million. Of course, the business may be currently at a total asset capacity of US$300,000. Making the goal precise helps you determine how much effort you need to put in to get your goal accomplished. And on a pre-determined time interval within the period of the goal-setting, an appraisal is done to check if progress is being recorded or not.

There are three types of goals: short-term, mid-term, and long-term. Short-term goals are to be met in one year or less; mid-term goal is scheduled for between one to five years and long-term goal is for five years or more. For instance, vacations, gifts, and electronics are typical short-term goals. A down payment for a house is a common mid-term goal. Long-term goals may include business growth and development, saving for retirement and a child's higher education.

Tracking your goals is essential. The Financial Goals Chart will help determine the timeline for your goals and the amount of money you'll need to regularly set aside in order to reach them. You may find the numbers daunting or even not realistic based on your current financial situation. You may be able to increase your income and/or decrease your expenses or have to consider adjusting your goals. Determining your priorities is essential. If you share your finances with someone else, discuss and set priorities together. It is not uncommon for couples to work at cross-purposes financially without even knowing it. By communicating with each other and determining what's most important, it will be much easier to reach your goals.

Taking stock of what your financial situation is today can help you determine what you need to do in order to prepare for tomorrow. Are you on the right track or do you need to make changes? Do you know exactly where your money is going each month? If not, you are not alone. Many of us are well aware of the symptoms of financial distress we are experiencing, such as having credit card debt, overdrawing a checking account, not being able to save, or paying bills late, but are not sure of the cause. Assessing your cash flow can help you figure that out.

Incomes are cash in-flows. The most common source of income is wages from a job, but it can also include things like investment earnings, child support, allowance, rental payments (if you are a landlord), government benefits, gifts, and profits from self-employment or a hobby. While gifts, child support, and some government benefits are generally not taxable, most income is. Your gross income is your income before taxes are taken out. Your net income is your income after taxes are taken out.

Expenses are cash out-flows. They can include essentials, such as mortgage or rent, food, and medical costs, as well as things you choose to spend money on, such as piano lessons and vacation. Savings can be considered an expense too – the money may not be leaving your hands, but you are setting it aside, and not to be used for other purposes.

Cash flow software can be used to list your income and expenses; and get accurate figures on where your money is going mostly. If your income exceeds your expenses, you have a positive cash flow. If your expenses exceed your income, you have a negative cash flow.

See the Big Picture Now

Tomorrow that you do not see today can never come. Financial success of US$ 10 million in the next five years will not be achievable without you first seeing it in your mind today. The mind is the tool we use for creative visualization, and therefore, it is essential to know of its capabilities. The mind is more of an energy unit activating the physical brain and making you aware of the environment around you. It gives you the awareness about yourself as an individual; and it is the tool with which you think, make decision and manage your life. So what do you see of yourself in the next five years? Still the way you are now with myriads of problems; or achieving your dreams, including financial success? If your predominant thoughts are negative, your subconscious mind will become programmed to see and expect problems, failure and unhappiness; and will also attract them into your life. If most of your thoughts are positive, your subconscious mind will assist you to see the positive and would attract success and happiness into your life.

Why Seeing the Big Picture Important?

In solving a mathematical function for a minimum error, there is the idea of local minima or maxima. Imagine it as a small hill or valley on a map. It might not be the highest or lowest point on the whole map, but in that small section of the map, it's the best height around. And it's a trap, locking the solution, or the person, into something other than the best possible result. This is what not seeing the big picture does to us. We constantly look at our feet, focusing on going uphill, until we reach the top. Then we look around and realize we've climbed up a small hill, surrounded by much larger hills. We'll have to go downhill, and then climb again to get to the highest peak.

However, if we have the vision to see the big picture from the beginning, we can see all the peaks in the area, and then plot a far more efficient route to get to that peak. We might even leave an escape route, in case we spot a higher peak on the way, right?

The same applies to life. What path are you pursuing, and how much effort are you putting into finding your best possible result? Is it a global maximum, or just a local one? Finding the highest peak might involve switching careers or even moving to somewhere that has more possibilities. But it relies on you having the vision to look for the big picture.

The question you should ask is "where can I apply this in my life?" We could make a list of people who had vision and saw the big picture. Captains of industry typically fall into such category. Getty, Rockefeller, Gates, Jobs, and so many others. Political leaders as well, from Gandhi and Churchill, to America's founders, to Alexander the Great, to Cincinnatus. These entire people saw the big picture and they were guided by it throughout their lives to the best possible spots of their existence. Along the way, things happened, some good and some not so well, but they had the vision to see where they could go, and how they were going to get there. And they made it happen.

While all the people listed above were players at the world stage, you don't need that high level profile to see the big picture. To have vision, to see where your life is going, that doesn't require you to be world-class, just be yourself. What are your hopes and aspirations? Where is your mountain top? What are you trying to maximize?

But how many of us are in the best possible job to get to where we want to go? To get to the next step in wealth, I would have to quit my job and become an entrepreneur. As a business owner, especially if one is successful, one can make a great deal of money more than as an employee. However, there are significant risks and down sides to being the boss. So I have achieved local maxima for my cash flow. However, I've learned that there are other ways to measure my success and my happiness, ways that don't require tons of cash. I am focusing on some of my effort on other routes to the highest hill of happiness I can see. How are you trying to get to the best place you can see? Are you focused on so small a portion of your life that you are not seeing the big picture, and all the other ways you can get what you are hoping for out of life? Do you have vision, or do you just see what's in front of your nose?

There are many paths, many routes, many ways, to get to financial happiness. Is your goal to be happy, or have you lost the big picture, and zoomed in on one route or method? Take a moment and look around at where you are, where you want to be, and why you want to be there. Once you have a better view of the big picture, you will start to gain the vision you need to find the better way, perhaps even the best way, to get there.

Power of Creative Mind on the Big Picture

Thought that you most often think have great effect on your behavior, actions and life. This means that you need to be aware of your thoughts; allow positive thoughts to envelope your mind and ensure no negative thoughts are permitted. When you repeat the same thought every day, your subconscious mind is programmed to seek for a way to bring it into reality. Thoughts and mental images, combines with your emotions, lead to an action, and the action leads to a fulfillment or accomplishment.

If you must take your business to the US$10 million mark in the next five years, it must start as a thought or mental image from your mind. Every building, invention or business somehow began in the mind as thought or mental image; and then brought into the physical by a strong desire. This implies that the external, physical world we see mirrors the inner worlds of thoughts and desires. I know of a particular frontline cleric who was always saying he cannot be poor when the annual turnover from his church was just US$ 105. But today, his ministry has the largest auditorium in the whole world. Our though and desires builds a subtle reality in the mental, feeling and emotional worlds. When repeated often, they gather enough strength to attract opportunities and to create the required environment to produce the clever realities we see in the physical world.

Creative visualization begins in the mental/feeling/emotional world, but its results are evident in the physical world. Hence, thought supply the aim, purpose and direction; and our desires add energy to it. If you consciously, choose the thoughts, phrases and words that you repeat in your mind, your life will start to change. You will begin creating new situations and circumstances. You will be using the power of assertions. Assertions are sentences that are repeated often, stating a particular desire or goal. These sentences sink into the subconscious mind, which in turn, releases enormous power to materialize the intention of the spoken word.

Here are a few positive assertions:
- I am a success and not a failure.

- I see my business producing turnover of US$ 10million in the next five years.
- A lot of money is flowing now into my life.
- The power of the universal mind is now filling my life with wealth.
- Healing energy is constantly filling every cell of my body.
- I remain calm and in control of my life, in every circumstances.
- Today is a wonderful and happy day for me.

Instead of repeating negative and useless words and phrases in the mind, choose positive words and phrases to help you build the life you want. In the environment where I grew up, there was a woman who is filled with negative words, and always uses the same for everyone that offends her. On a particular day, she told her son to get her a spoon from the kitchen, and the son brought knife instead. Her word to the boy was "I think you are knocked down by a car?". The boy ran back to the kitchen and brought spoon to the mother as demanded. It was early morning when this incident took place; the boy went to school as usual. However, the woman's pronouncement came into effect in the afternoon when the boy was returning home from school. A car actually knocked down the boy. When she was told of what has happened to her son, then she screamed "my enemy is after me again". When I heard her scream, I said the evil seed you sowed in the life of your son in the early morning has germinated and bear fruit for you.

There is this gardener also who was employed by a man to assist him in keeping his premises in order. He was given a room at the boy's quarter with his family. From day one that the man and his family packed into the room; each morning before going out of the room he will make a pronouncement that he is a landlord and not a tenant, and that soon he will soon be taking rent on his own house. This he keeps declaring each passing day. Seven years has now passed, yet he is still in the one room at the boy's quarter. However, nature heard him each time he made the pronouncement. In the ninth year, something miraculous happened; his master received a transfer letter to go to another continent where the company had a branch office, and the notice was so sudden and short that he had to leave immediately. So he called his gardener and informed him of the posting; and asked if he wants to buy the house.

The gardener answered him and said "sir you know how much you are paying me? I can never afford it." But as a result of the short notice for the landlord to report at his new station, he asked the gardener how much does he have? He said it's just US$120. The landlord collected the money from him and passed all the house documents to him. Truly, he packed into the main house and rented the boy's quarter out. So his declaration from day one of packing into the house came to past. He became a landlord indeed.

By choosing your thoughts and words you exercise control over your life and destiny. We define our tomorrow positively or negatively by the mental picture created in our mind today and what pronouncement we make on those mental picture continually. Therefore, what we see today is as a result of our thought and actions yesterday. Tomorrow's success and affluence can be created by engaging our mind today on those things we want to see happen.

Handling Challenges on Your Way

Arriving at your destination when you embark on the journey to financial freedom is anchored on your resolve to demolish challenges off your way anytime you become aware of any. There are battles to fight in order to get your financial success crown released to you. Ask any financially successful man how he got his financial fortune and you will hear some tales you've never heard before. Tribulation is bound to come but the assurance I have for you is that if you face it doggedly, you will overcome every one of them.

When challenges come your way do not be despair, rather be determined to overcome it. To be a champion, you have to see the big picture and work at it until you can handle it. It doesn't end with just seeing the big picture alone, getting to the big picture is much more important. Handling the big picture is handling challenges that want to stop you from reaching it. It's not about winning and losing; it's about every day hard work and about thriving on a challenge. It's about embracing the pain that you'll experience at the end of a race and not being afraid. People think too hard and get afraid of challenge.

I work really hard at trying to see the big picture and not getting stuck in ego. I believe we're all put on this planet for a purpose, and we all have a different purpose... When you connect with that love and that compassion, that's when everything unfolds. If your focus is on the smallest details, you never get the big picture right.

The reality, I believe, is the fact that all change starts small anyway. The big picture is just too gigantic, too unfathomable and seemingly immovable if we attempt to swallow it at once. But it gives us idea of something to expect, quantifiable and personalize–able and, suddenly, our perspective shifts in that direction. The big picture doesn't just come from distance; it also takes time. In order to properly understand the big picture, everyone should fear becoming mentally fogged up and obsessed with one small section of its truth. Therefore, you can overcome that challenge; all that is required is courage and moving on. Courage as it will interest you to know is not freedom over fear; it is being afraid and going on.

4

YOUR DECISION TO BE AMAZING at something is not determined by skill or aptitude, **IT'S DETERMINED BY YOUR ATTITUDE.**

Never Remain Idle

An idle mind is the devils workshop is a popular saying today. An idle mind has high degree of probability to engage negative behavior. Human energy can be channeled in two directions; for positive endeavor which yields positive results; and negative endeavor, which produces negative results. Choosing to stay positive in stressful situations isn't about fooling yourself; it's about understanding that negativity is a waste of energy. Tomorrow will be what you make it to be today. It can be filled with lack, disappointments, and fear. Or you can turn it around and make it a day filled with plenty, joy, and hope. You get to choose. Dear reader, there are two things I'll like to emphasize in this chapter about succeeding financially. One is right attitude and the other is radiating right thoughts. You may be very diligent, but wrong attitude could rub you of successful financial destiny.

A lazy grasshopper laughed at a little ant as she was always busy gathering food in the summer. "Why are you working so hard?" he asked, "come into the sunshine and listen to my merry notes". But the ant went on her work. She said" I am laying in store for the winter. Sunny days won't last forever." The grasshopper answered, "winter is so far away, so take it easy". And when the winter came, the ant settled down in her snug house. She had plenty of food to last the whole winter. The grasshopper had nothing to eat so he went to the ant and begged her for a little corn. "No", replied the ant, "you laughed at me when I worked in the summer. You yourself sang throughout the summer; so it is better for you to dance away the winter."

Right Attitude

Friends, one of the pillars to financial success is right attitude. What is your attitude when input is required from you and no financial remuneration is involved? Graduates (both colleges and universities) today are so much interested in starting big, rather than starting with something small first, no matter how small it is. To those that are money conscious and myopic in mind, engaging their hands in something small is not an option; not to mention the phrase "without pay". Their whole body system reacts immediately against it. Many believed in the government's social security funds instead; this of course, puts some stipends in the pocket of the jobless. What happens if your country does not operate social security benefits? If you say there is no job, have you attempt to work for free in an organization where your interest lies? Thomas was a university graduate in electrical engineering, and has roamed the job market for more than five years. At a point he decided to offer his skills for free. The reason for this is to avoid staying at home or roaming the street the whole day with nothing to show for it. He signed up with a company that sells and repair electric pumps, an area he is familiar. Initially, he was rejected on the condition that the company was not doing well and so cannot afford to pay his salary. Instead of choosing to stay at home or roam the street, Thomas agreed to work for this company without pay. He was told to resume work the following week, and was placed under a supervisor. Within six months of working with the company he became a specialist in pump repair, performing better than the actual staff. With this result, his supervisor made a case for him during one of the management meetings for allowance to be paid to him. This was approved and the amount could hardly pay his transport to and from work for one month. Even with this he was not deterred; rather he gave his unwavering commitment to the job assigned to him. In his ninth month in the company, an important message came from his village that his father just passed away and he would have to be at the burial. He sought permission from his supervisor to attend his father's burial which will last up to one week. His permission was granted, so he travelled to the village for the burial. It was as if his father's death was orchestrated by a divine plan; while in the village, his company got a lot of pump servicing jobs which could not be handled by his staffed colleagues. The supervisor made a case to the management for the pump to be serviced by a near-by company pending the return of Thomas. All incoming jobs on pump repairs were sent to this company, and Thomas' company paid a lot of money on the pump servicing. At this point, the manager got to know that all the other regular staff could not handle the pump repair. It was in one of the management meetings that the manager asked Thomas' supervisor what he was being paid; and he responded that it was just some allowance. There in the meeting, Thomas' salary was decided. And guess what? He was made the assistant supervisor.

Dear reader, to succeed financially, despise not the days of small beginning. Thomas could have remained in the wilderness of joblessness if he refuses the offer of work without pay. It takes time to succeed! This is why it's critical to work in an area that you love! It will serve you well to do something that you thoroughly enjoy, something that you're passionate about. It's your love that will allow you to continue with work when everyone else has gone home; it is your passion that will drive you to the finish line. There was a time when Michael Jordan never scored in a basketball game; there was a time when Bill Gates wasn't exactly sure how to create the Windows operating system. But through failure, determination, time and experience success was born. See something great in your small beginning, the giant oak tree slumbers in the acorn, the bald eagle waits patiently in the egg. If you are consistent, and if you commit to putting in the time, you will become an expert, and it is your expertise that is the doorway to your financial success.

Radiating Right Thoughts

The behavior people see around you is once your thought. The thoughts that you repeatedly think shape your life. To succeed financially, you must imbibe the right thoughts. It is what you think in your mind that manifest in the physical. This is what people see from the outside about you. People who have entertained negative thoughts and feelings most of their lives, expect failure and do not feel positioned for success. If they have experienced lack and hardships, they believe that success is not for them. In this case, everything associated with success might evoke negative feelings. Your thoughts and feelings can draw or repel success. They shape your beliefs and expectations about success or failure. Thoughts too often, come and go and change direction like the wind. They influence your mind the same way that the wind affects the direction of a flag. One moment the flag may be fluttering this way, and a moment later in a different direction. One moment you might be thinking one thing or see things from a certain viewpoint, and a moment later this can change.

Man is made or unmade by himself; in the armory of thoughts and actions, he forges the weapons by which he destroys himself; fashion the tools with which he builds for himself heavenly mansions of success, joy, strength and peace. By the right choice and true application of thoughts, man builds for himself financial success, lasting harmony with his environment, and ultimate contentment. Equally, by the abuse and wrong application of thoughts, he descends below the level of a beast. Between these two extremes are all the grade of characters we see on the earth; and man is the maker and master of it all.

Consider the following story: there were two dogs, both at separate times walk into the same room. One comes out shaking his tail while the other comes out barking angrily. A man watching the two dogs goes into the room to see what could possibly make one dog so happy and the other despondent. To his surprise, he discovered a room filled with several mirrors. The happy dog found a thousand happy dogs looking back at him smiling, so he smiles back; while the angry dog saw several angry dogs seriously angry with him, which made him to be angry too.

Reader, my question to you is *"what projection are you giving of yourself to people around you?"* There is a proverb that says the way people see you is the way they address you. If you make yourself responsible and presentable before the people you meet daily; even though you are a nonentity, they will only know when they hear you speak. Mostly, human beings judge by outward appearance rather than any inward attributes. Know the success potential that you carry inside of you and exhume this confidence to the outside world, and you will be given that level of respect. I have seen a poor man who has no starting capital, but won series of contacts as a result of his confidence at all time. During the interview for his first contract, the interviewers were so astonished by his level of confidence that he was tipped for the contract when he had no money to supply the needed items. Friends, radiate clean positive thoughts in your mind, and it will soon be seen on the outside. Your predominant habitual thoughts and feelings determine whether you will achieve success or not, and whether you will feel satisfied upon realization or not. This means that you have to be more aware of your thoughts and feelings. It is important to learn to be more positive, less critical, and less worried. Then, when success is achieved, you can enjoy the happiness of achievement. Thoughts, attitudes and habits can be changed. The change does not come overnight anyway; some inner work is necessary. Positive thoughts and feelings make you happier and more receptive to success, and a positive disposition bestows upon you the ability to enjoy success when it comes.

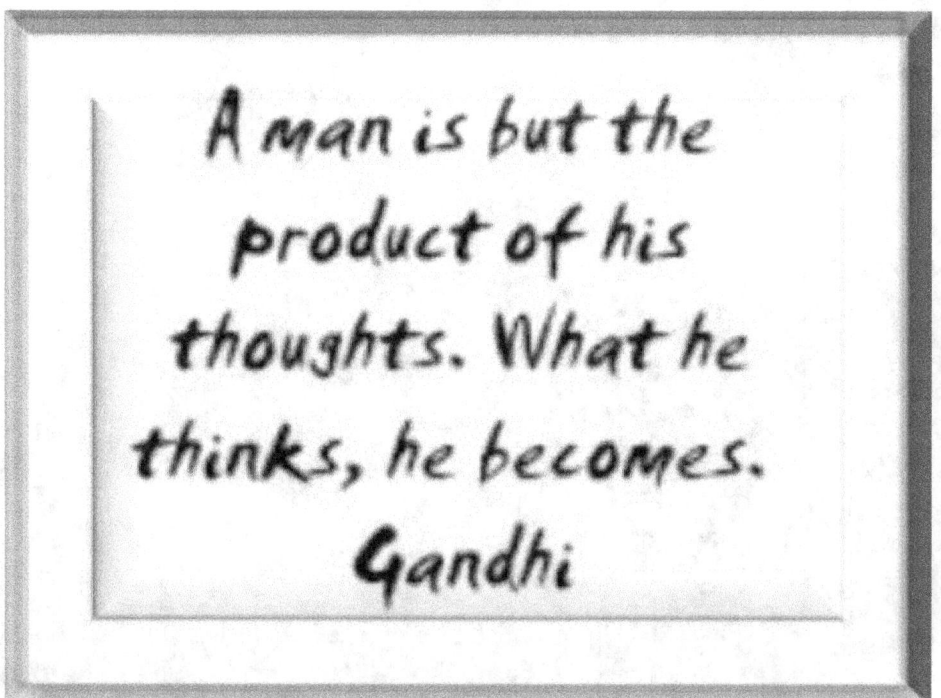

Take it as a challenge, and pay more consideration to your thoughts and feelings. Try and find out what kind of thoughts you think and what kind of feelings you usually experience in connection with the thoughts. If your thoughts and feelings are positive that's fine. But if you think and feel failure, unhappiness and dissatisfaction always, then you need to do something about it. Why is it that people desire success? There is a desire for growth in each one of us. It is the cosmic desire for expression and expansion. This desire manifests in every form of life. We see it everywhere, even in a blade of grass, which can grow on a rock or on a wall. The desire for success is the inner natural desire for growth, expansion and expression.

Financial Empowerment Training

Financial empowerment implies providing basic financial literacy to people who have the ability to make informed decisions about their own finances, to spot a shady deal when they see one, and to make financial plans for their future and budget accordingly. Readers are leaders! Knowledge is key in defeating any force of opposition in life. To succeed in any area of life you need sufficient knowledge or information on that aspect. Boost your chance of financial success through attending seminars, workshops, and reading related materials on financial success. Many have achieved financial success ahead of you, so what did they do to climb this ladder of success? There are expert articles and reports in the libraries and all over the Internet that can put you on the pedestal of success financially.

When you are new to operating any business, it's natural to take one look at the amount of resources you can find on the web, and as a result get overwhelmed. For instance, if you are in the area of Internet marketing business; so many options are available to you: do I go for pay-per-check advertising? Online classified ad sites? Banner exchanges? Should you get a website of your own? And so on. However, one thing you must also note is that not all information you see on the web may meet your need. So you have to be selective in order not to collect junks of material that may poison your resolve of financial success. If you are a novice on Internet income for example, an Internet income course could take you specifically through the nitty-gritty of what is involve in Internet income business and how you could put yourself on a good start with some ideas from the experts that will take you through the step-by-step processes of the complex world of online marketing in plain language that's easy to understand.

To be an effective Internet marketer, you need to analyze and understand Internet traffic and, very importantly, you must understand that the "traffic" consists of human beings with unique feelings and interests and desires. You must understand that they are looking for what they want to find--not what you want them to find. You must understand that they will get there through their methods--not the methods you may prefer for them to use. The old broadcast media methods of controlling attention do not work so well on the Internet. It's a new ball game altogether now. You must use valuable content and ease of use to create flow. You must properly position your site within the flow of Internet traffic. Once you get this right, you are on the road to becoming a very successful Internet entrepreneur.

On the other hand, if your business enjoys more physical representation with less web presence; financial empowerment training will help put your business on a strong financial footing. You don't have to know everything about financial planning or investments to be financially successful. You can pay an expert to lend a hand to you on challenging questions that are specific to your business situation and help you with investing. The harder part is to have savings that continues to build and grow. Unfortunately, there is no "hot" stock tip that is going to make you millions at once.

Develop Personal Financial Empowerment Strategies

Becoming financially capable is a critical step toward establishing financial success and security, particularly for low-income, financially-handicapped entrepreneurs. Financial empowerment strategies involves personally developed pre-established financial capability building programs that will assist you on where you can receive funding advice and technical assistance to help you refine and expand your business. Technical assistance includes both one-on-one coaching and peer-learning opportunities. By managing your expenses, establishing long-term goals; and effectively navigating the financial support and income services available, you can put yourself in a better position to stay on in business and establish healthy financial behaviors.

A friend of mine on a salaried job presented his monthly budget to me one day and it shows he should be saving a good portion of his salary every month. But the fact is at the end of the month, he is already waiting for the current month's salary to come so as to meet some expenses. So what it means is that money is going towards things that are not listed on his budget. I told him the way to get answers to this problem is to track his spending and go back and see what he actually spent money on over the past month. Those that are irrelevant or frivolous in nature can be avoided. To succeed financially you must exercise a high level of financial discipline at all times. There are people I had met overtime, and all you can see around them is I feel like having this; I feel like having that. Everything they set their eyes on they want to have. I find it difficult to understand how someone who has been on a salary of US$2,500 monthly for one year in a developing country does not have any savings. Rather he comes to borrow from those that even earn much less. Being meticulous in your spending will determine if you can achieve financial success or not in the future.

Some people are borrowing agents. No matter what they earn, it is never enough; they still borrow. To make matter worst, they borrow from people who earn far less than they do. Rather they will class you who are careful with your spending as the stingy type. So it suffice to say that what you earn do not determine your financial success in life, but your financial discipline. People in this category as a matter of urgency should register themselves as soon as possible for financial empowerment training available at their neighborhood.

Engage Prudent Financial Planning

Personal financial planning is controlling your everyday financial affairs to enable you to do the things that bring you financial accomplishment and satisfaction. A balanced approach to spending and saving is essential in the pursuit of financial freedom. If balancing the two will give you some headache, then you need the service of a financial advisor.

However, before engaging the dotted line with a new financial advisor be sure to ask about his/her strategies. It's likely that you'll feel more comfortable with an advisor whose strategies are simple and easy to understand. It can be devastating to get advice from someone who discusses your goals and investment objectives with confusing charts, terminology, and presentations. Simple and easy to understand is best. You will also want to ensure your financial advisor is communicative and will keep you updated on a regular basis with easy-to-understand information. If the issue of financial advisor is confirmed, the first step in personal financial planning is controlling your day-to-day financial dealings to enable you to do the things that will take you to the big picture. This is achieved by planning and following a budget. The second step is choosing and following an itinerary toward long-term financial goals. As with anything else in life, without financial goals and specific plans for meeting them, you can drift along the way and leave your future to chance. A wise man once

40

said: *"most people don't plan to fail; they just fail to plan."* The end result is the same: failure to reach financial independence.

Four Simple Steps to Setting Viable Financial Goals

Financial management is the process of managing the financial resources, including accounting and financial reporting, budgeting, collecting accounts receivable, risk management, and insurance for a business. The financial management system for a small business includes both how you are financing it as well as how you manage the money in the business. Buoyant financial management requires setting lofty financial goals and putting plans in place to accomplish them. The following steps are relevant in setting good financial goals:

Step 1: Identify and write down your financial goals, whether they are for business investment, buying a new car, saving toward a down payment on a house etc.

Step 2: Break each financial goal down into several short-term (less than 1 year), medium-term (1 to 3 years) and long-term (5 years or more) goals.

Step 3: Educate yourself! Read money magazine or a book about investment. With a little effort you can learn enough to make educated decisions that will increase your net worth many times over. Then identify small, measurable steps you can take to achieve these goals, and put this action plan to work.

<u>Step 4:</u> Evaluate your improvement. Review your progress monthly, quarterly, or at any other interval you feel comfortable with, but at least semi-annually, to determine if your program is working. If you're not making satisfactory progress on a particular goal, re-evaluate your approach and make changes as necessary.

Financial Success Toolkit ...*Launchpad Series*
http://royalseedsinternational.blogspot.com/

6

Risk–Taking and Financial Success

Risk taking is an integral part of business and life, but only few people know how to manage it properly. The word risk has a slightly negative implication to it — it implies danger, tension, and possible loss. But risk also has a positive side, the chance of hitting a big win, of getting

43

more on the back side than you invest on the front side. It is a known fact that every great leap forward in human life begins with risk-taking and a giant step of faith into the unknown. Men and women who achieve goals and accomplish wonderful things are invariably men and women of great faith in themselves and their abilities. The better you become at analyzing and assessing before taking a risk, and then avoiding as much of the risk as possible, the more competent and more capable you will become, and the more successful you will be.

Risk-taking is inseparable from financial success. In actual fact, everything about life is risk; whenever you engage in any action where the outcome is uncertain, you are taking a risk. You are taking a risk whenever you venture into the unknown, where your possibilities and probabilities cannot be determined to an exact degree. From the time you get up in the morning until you go back to bed at night, and even when you are sleeping, you are taking a risk to some degree. It is how skillful and confident you are in taking the right risks for the right reasons to achieve goals that determines your success.

In the same way, firms that gains competitive advantage from risk taking do not do so by accident. In the process of doing business, it is inevitable that you will be faced with unexpected and often unpleasant surprises that threaten to undercut and even destroy your business. That is the essence of risk and how you respond to it will determine whether you survive and succeed. In fact, there are key elements that successful risk-taking organizations have in common. First, they succeed in aligning the interests of their decision makers (managers) with the owners of the business (shareholders) so that firms expose themselves to the right risks and for the right reasons. Second, they choose the right people for the task; some individuals respond to risk better than others. Finally, the culture of the organizations is conducive to sensible risk taking and it is structured accordingly. If there is a key to successful risk taking, it is to ensure that those who expose a business to risk or respond to risk; make their decisions with a common purpose in mind, and that is to increase the value of their businesses. If the interests of the decision makers are not aligned with those who own the business, it becomes inevitably clear that the business will be exposed to some risks that it should not have been exposed to.

Generally, in the world of investments and business; the importance of spreading one's risks is essential. No individual or company should be dependent upon one or two people for their financial well-being. One of the best ways to minimize risk-taking is to develop alternatives to what you are currently doing. The more alternatives you have, the lower your risk, and the higher the likelihood to achieve goals and reach your success in life. Having a number of alternative business or personal plans at your disposal therefore is a shock absorber in your pursuit of financial success.

Intelligent and Calculated Risks Reduces Your Pain

Please note that there is nowhere in the world where you'll always have what you want each time you take risk; but you can reduce the number of failures if intelligently calculated. The ability to achieve your set goals in financial success will be affected by the risk taking strategies you use in all areas of your life. You learn how to take intelligent risks without fear by taking a risk cleverly and then analyzing what happened is essential in getting to your goals. When you have clearly identified the risk involved, you can plan and prepare to maximize your opportunities while minimizing those risks. Intelligent and calculated risks will reduce the pains of negative results; this is because most of such risks will bring positive energy to you. Your ability to confidently take calculated risks in the direction of your goals will ultimately help you achieve goals you set for yourself and lead you toward success in life.

Good risk takers have a combination of traits that seem mutually exclusive. They are realists who still manage to be optimistic; they tend to be realistic in their assessments of success and failure but they are also confident in their capacity to deal with the consequences.

They allow for the possibility of losses but are not overwhelmed or scared by its prospects; in other words, they do not allow the possibility of losses to tilt their decision–making processes. They are able to both keep their perspective and see the big picture even as they are immersed in the details of a crisis; in terms of decision making, they frame decisions widely and focus in on those details that have large consequences. Finally, they can make decisions with limited and often incomplete information; and make reasonable assumptions about the missing pieces.

Avoid Procrastinations

The saying that '*procrastination is the thief of time*' is real. Time is an essential aspect of life for every human being. Time once misused, is lost forever. Usually, your time for a particular thing elapses if you are either late or postpone doing it. The more you delay or procrastinate, the more you tend to lose out on the benefits that should follow the fulfillment of that event. After all, time is money as we all know.

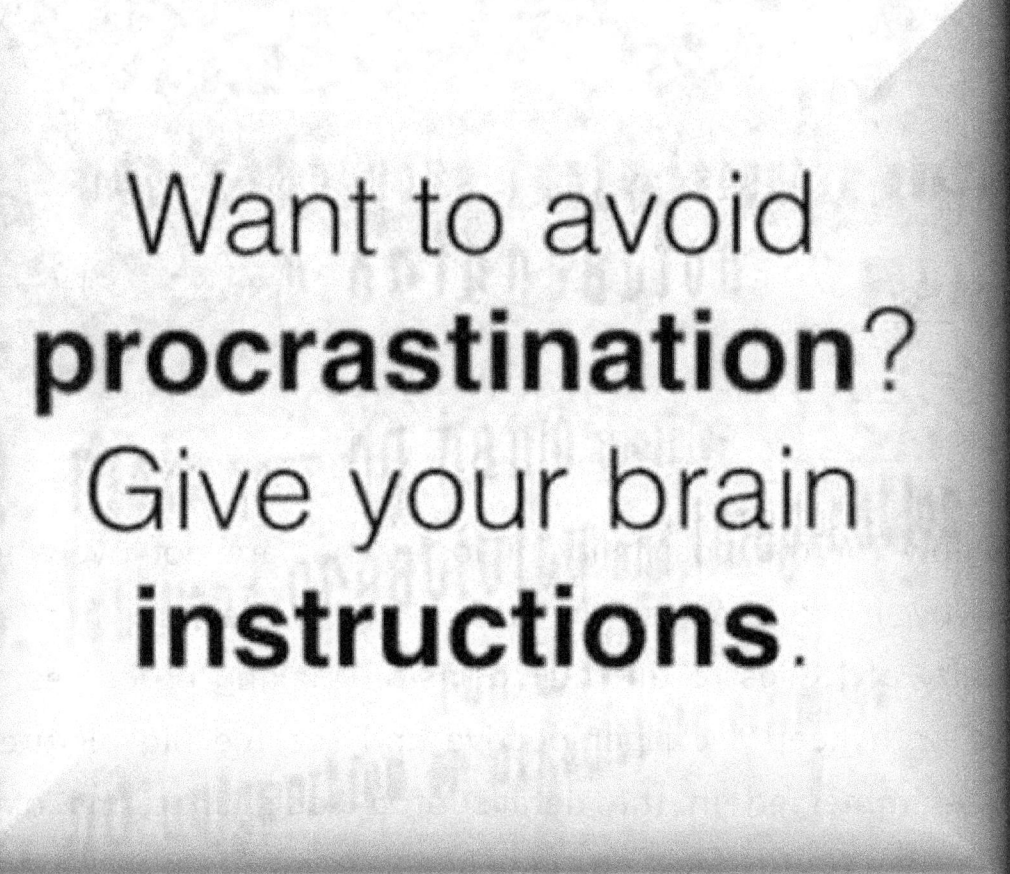

Want to avoid **procrastination?** Give your brain **instructions**.

Time is a jewel that is inexplicable – a mystery we must set out to find out. By procrastinating, you are rescheduling the things in your live that shouldn't necessarily be overlooked. Putting things off robs you of the opportunity to accomplish it. Time used in a wrong way is lost forever and it cannot be retrieved. Therefore the proverb *'procrastination is the thief of time'* is one adage whose words are effective and truthful in real life. If you are punctual at doing things on time or before time, you are a respected member of society. The ability to remain consistent with your choice is a proficiency that necessitates a lot of will-power. Choosing not to procrastinate requires exceptional principles, self-discipline and vigorous determination of the mind. One who does not procrastinate will be more successful in life emotionally, physically and mentally.

My counsel to you is to never do tomorrow what you can do today. It will be pretty difficult to start the next chapter of your life if you keep re-reading the last one. The best way to get something done is to begin. Do not wait; the time will never be just right to do what you plan to do. Start where you are, and work with whatever tools you have, and better tools will be found as you progress along the way. Every second is a chance to turn your life around for good. You don't always get what you wish for, but you get what you work for.

Tracking Your Achievements Keep You Going

The energy to keep moving on is derived from the past successes achieved. To have this energy, track your past achievements. The important thing is just to do it. The only way to get this done is to take the time and effort to follow up your achievement in detail. Congratulate yourself on each achievement.

What you achieve today should gear you up to greater heights in your exploit to financial dominion. Like any system, it only works if you work it, but so far I've been working it. I highly recommend this system, as it's a great way to keep you going on the track of financial success, and is a motivating factor towards achieving those goals.

Don't Hold on Your Negative Past

Reminiscence on the past to see how many successes and failures you have recorded. Keeping track of them will let you know the degree of success achieved so far and the area where you need to do some adjustments. However, don't let the negative pasts hold you back. Definitely, sometimes you may fall short of your expectation, that doesn't translate to be the end of the world for you; rather you should put on the guard of courage and move on with life. While positive past is a good reminiscence on which to build extra energy for the future, negative past contributes nothing to your well-being than to stop your progress. The only part of the past you should hold on is your good memories that can keep you better prepared for your next level encounter in life. When you hold on the past, you are missing the present. What you did yesterday brought you to where you are today; and it cannot be altered anymore. We hold ourselves back in ways both big and small, by lacking self-confidence and believe in ourselves. What you do with today is what determines your tomorrow.

Refuse to be Defeated

Defeat first begins in your mind before physically revealed. My advice to you is to ensure you don't allow it take root in your heart. It could destroy all that have been built in the past. Most people quickly get overthrown by the force of defeat, and therefore give up. "*I haven't failed. I've found 10,000 ways that don't work.*" This statement was credited to Thomas Edison, the inventor of the first commercial light bulb. If you have a goal of what you have set to achieve, keep up with the vision. It is something obvious, that each passing day that do not produce positive energy towards achieving your goal can bring frustration your way; I will advice you don't give up. It is an exceptional thing in life to take a leap at success of any kind the first time and achieve it.

If you have no confidence in self, you are twice defeated in the race of life. With confidence, you have won even before you have started.

But rather than allow the force of defeat to overtake you, each failed attempt should be seen as one of the many ways that things should not be done. So retrace your steps and start all over. Those failed attempts have added to your experience in that area of endeavor, and therefore teaches you not to go in that direction anymore. If you don't accept defeat, for sure you will not give up.

Continuous Improvement Lifestyle

Financial success may be likened to a garden which is intelligently cultivated and monitored to prevent weeds from choking the plant. A garden that is left alone, whether cultivated or neglected, must and will bring forth. If no useful seeds are continuously sown into it, an abundance of useless weeds will produce their kinds and make the farm grow wild. Just as a gardener continue to cut the weeds in his farm from time to time to allow desired plants to get enough nutrients for growth and survival, so must we continue to strive for financial

53

success and better life. What we achieve today was as a result of the effort of yesterday; the effort of today will make way for the success of tomorrow. Not to cultivate any effort in the direction of our financial goal today is to expect nothing tomorrow.

To keep yourself on the track of financial success continuously, you have to keep improving on the success of today. The motor industries will give a good analogy on continuous improvement. For instance, a vehicle manufacture by Ford motor company in the 1960s was very valuable at that time because it is the best effort around then. The same vehicle if reproduced and sold to the market today will receive much less patronage from buyers, if not none. Each year, motor manufacturers follow market trends and buyers desires to produce the next series. Human tastes are changing continuously, and so must the manufacturer respond to this taste in order to get for their products, good share of the market. In all human endeavors there are exertions, and the strength of the exertion is the measure of the result you should expect.

There was this classmate of mine when I was in secondary school. He was the only child of his parents then, and much care and attention was given to him so he could get the best out of life. Because the parents were anxious to see him grow to become a child of reference among his equals, they sought to know about his tomorrow today. They consulted an oracle priest who confirmed to them that their son will be king of his town in the near future. The parents rather than keep the information to them and continue to encourage the young lad on his way to success; chose to divulge the future success envisioned by the oracle priest to the boy.

As soon as the boy received the good news, he was totally relaxed from his studies. Before then, he was one of the very good students in class. But after he was told about his future success as a king, he picks the bragging option. He was always telling us his classmates, "*ao you know whether I study or not I will be your king, and I will judge all of you as I want*". Readers; that time the king of our village were predominantly illiterates, and the two things required to be a king were just prudence and previous experiences of the individual in managing community matters. Friends, to cut the long story short; while we gained admission into the university, our future king colleague was a dropout. True to the oracle priest's prediction, it came to the time for a new king to be enthroned; and the kingmakers were looking for possible candidates in the family house of our classmate. His name was chosen among the many possible candidates for the throne. Guest what my reader? He was overwhelmingly selected at first based on popularity. But in the second stage of the process he was eliminated on the ground that he was an illiterate, and the kingmaker made it clear to him that gone were the days when popularity alone can earn a man the kingship. And that today, due to the enormous roles of kings in public functions, an educated individual should be selected. So he lost his chance because he chose not to have a vision and improve on himself. Whatever you achieve as success today if not improved upon will be outdated in the near future. Your financial success now is only good for today, and if not improved upon, will become outdated in no distant future.

Conduct Research and Seek Advice

Successful financial management lifestyle is an ongoing process. It is important to continually monitor your spending, savings, and investments and adjust your plan as necessary. On a motivating note, you don't have to be an expert in financial management to achieve financial success, but a good understanding of the basics will help you; and put you in control of your money.

Financial matters, while very much a part of our lives, can be complicated at times. If you feel a little lost in some areas of personal finance, call upon an expert for help. There is no shame in not knowing everything. After all if you're sick, you go to a doctor; if your car breaks down, you take it to a mechanic. Financial planners, investment advisors, credit counselors, and insurance agents are examples of the types of financial experts that you can get help from.

You can also continue to learn on your own. An article on investments could be by a certified financial planner. There are a multitude of books and periodicals on personal finance, and many of them can be found at the library, so you don't even need to buy them. Dreamers are the savior of the world. The visible world is governed by the invisible; dream lofty dreams. And as you dream, so you will become. Your vision is the promise of what you will become one day. Your idea is the prophecy of what you shall at last unveil.

Take Advantage of Opportunities

Taking advantage of opportunities in life starts with simply saying yes to them when they come around; opportunities are not always exclusive to an individual, rather they are open to many. Others might be tempted to move in on them if they stumble on it. If you hesitate, you may lose out. Decision–making is what delay taking advantage of opportunities. While taking your time to make decision on an issue, you should also be aware that your decision is time constrained. If longer than necessary, it may cost you a great deal of regret. Great opportunities often come from your own enormous ideas, so seat down and think. If you're negative about yourself, you'll just limit possible options available to you. This is not a good state of mind to be in.

Opportunities and risk-taking often go together. If you cannot take risk, it is certain that opportunities will always pass you by. Someone who is a great risk-taker is sure to succeed; if that success is not seen around him now, give it time it will come. There is no way you can cage a risk-takers success; it will always come to be. The best opportunity is often the riskiest. Someone starting up a new business is not only taking a risk, but also taking advantage of an opportunity. Door of opportunities are never closed, and is not limited to the business field alone. You can look for, create, and take advantage of opportunities within your profession. Keep in mind not all opportunities result in promotions. They may be new challenges or increased responsibilities. It may allow you to gain experience, or prove to others your various skills and abilities. Opportunities do not guarantee an immediate increase in pay, and may require more work in the short term. Too many times employees miss out on opportunities because it requires more work for the same pay. What they do not realize is that their manager is giving them an opportunity to learn a new skill or demonstrate the ability to perform a task, either of which would make them eligible candidate for promotion in the future.

While not all opportunities come with financial rewards attached, they may instead offer you the ability to learn, develop, and demonstrate new skills which may be required for future promotion. Unfortunately, employees sometime miss out on these opportunities because there was no immediate or instant gratification attached to it. Instead, they consider the extra workload as a detriment instead of an opportunity. Understandably, everyone wants to make more money, and wants to get paid for their effort; taking on extra responsibilities is an investment in your career. As someone possibly new to the corporate world, you should concentrate on building your resume for future job advancement. Most employers want individuals with experience for higher level positions. By assigning added responsibilities, supervisors are providing their employees with a way to obtain this experience

Financial Success Toolkit …*Launchpad Series*
http://royalseedsinternational.blogspot.com/

while still maintaining their current position. Consider it to be on-the-job training for your future job. While excelling in new responsibilities such as preparing a report or creating a work schedule do not give any monetary rewards at present, you are gaining valuable experience which makes you more promotable in the future. When interviewing for a future job which lists "ability to create a work schedule" as a job requirement, you can confirm you not only have the ability, you also have the experience. You took the opportunity to proactively become more promotable instead of waiting for the promotion to come to you.

My advice is to take advantage of every opportunity you are given in an organization or that comes your way in the course of business. On the job activities, training classes, books, and the internet are all excellent ways to learn and grow. Demonstrating the initiative to learn new responsibilities will make you promotable, if not at your current job, then at another company. Also, take the time to make your own opportunities. Instead of waiting for opportunity to come knocking on your door, you could also drive over to opportunity's house instead. Once you have conquered your normal work duties, ask your supervisor for additional responsibilities. Managers love employees who show initiative. Use these opportunities as a stepping stone for better things to come.

Principles of Sustainable Business and World of Opportunities

Opportunities are short-lived. You need to be quick in order to get the most out of them. The business world of today is filled with turbulence. And according to experts, turbulence rather than tranquility is the normal expectation of most business owners. As a matter of fact when business brings profit continuously for the owner over a range of time, he is surprise. This is because in the business arena, you have a world that is unstable and complicated, and requires more focus on what your employees and customers think, feel, want and need. Call it a slow down or a recession, the impact is the same – times are challenging. Today's business world requires effectiveness with change, strong communication and full awareness of every detail of your business. You must live by a strategic plan, one that is clear, focused, accountable and empirical. You must rally your organization to be on the go for opportunities – to review every aspect of business, consider every situation, know trends, needs and challenges – and respond with ways to add value.

Five main principles that can sustain your business on the pedestal of success are outlined below. Build these principles into your business culture and you will have the formula to succeed; moreover, attract and retain the best employees and customers in your area of business:

1. Expect change, either positive or negative and learn to welcome it; it is the only constant thing on this planet.
2. Know your business: know your purpose, core strengths, and everything about your customers and competitors.
3. Share what you know; eliminate all obstacles; engage in open and honest communication.
4. Learn to focus on opportunities; be flexible; approach each day with optimism to see ways to create value and improve your efficiencies.

5. Own your success; build a plan and work it out each day.

You are now aware that change is constant and it can be your greatest source of drive for growth and improvement. Things change, and today's challenges are just another component of the changes that every business must face. But the real issue isn't the change itself – it is how you welcome, use and respond to change. To be successful in a changing world you must re-consider much of what you took for granted in the past; you must become better at inventing, responding, communicating, sharing and staying focused on your core strengths. In every way, you must be great at the hunt for opportunities.

You should also have detailed information about your business – what works well and what needs improvement. Look for ways to improve on how you source and share information easily, completely and effectively with your teams. Opportunity-thinking is a significant component of every successful organization's culture; it is how they approach each day. With all these, the stage is set for your business or organization to welcome every opportunity that comes.

Self-Discipline and Financial Success

Self-discipline is a necessary skill for building and sustaining financial success. Without it you can never acquire or accumulate anything in life nor accomplish financial breakthrough of any respected magnitude. Generally, self-discipline is the ability to say no when you need to, and to be able to keep your emotions in check when there is need for such decision. It is being able to do the things you don't want to do when you know you must do it in order to achieve important life goals – financial stability and success. It is forcing yourself to do things that are necessary in both your financial and non-financial life.

One of the many contested tool that pushes people into debt dungeon today is the credit card. By the way, credit card companies saw the advantage of making life easier for the people, and so invented credit card. It is most unfortunate to think that credit card is an evil tool of wealth destruction. Credit cards are not evil tools of wealth destruction as many thinks. They don't automatically get people deep into debt. But the cardholder's high level of financial indiscipline brought them neck-deep into debt. Of course, if there is no discipline by the cardholder, debt will surely be incurred. I would rather blame that on the cardholder, not the credit card. It's not like the credit card walks into a store on two legs and starts making purchases!

By the same token, if somebody brings in a decent amount of income, some of it should be saved. It's not like most people are required to deplete their paycheck to pay for everything they want. Perhaps much of it goes towards things that are needed, but not necessarily for things that are simply wanted. For example, it's not like a person is possessed by some force of nature for the purpose of buying a luxury car. Or, it's not like one is forced and dragged to a store to buy a new pair of expensive shoes. The reality is that we all have the ability to make the right choices. In terms of spending choice, most of us know what to do. It isn't that complicated. Spend less than you make, resulting in some savings, which you can then invest. With absolute financial self-discipline, someday in the future you will achieve financial freedom. Even if that doesn't happen so easily, at least you can live a life that's responsible.

The key to all this is self–discipline. If you simply learn how to control yourself and make good choices, it will happen. The main thing is making the right choices every day, so that over time you build up strong financial habits and an equally solid income stream and portfolio of savings and investments. Make the right choices every day, and you are on your way to financial success.

Sometime in 1998 after graduating from the university and couldn't get a job immediately; I put up with my brother who owns a computer sales and repair outfit. I made up my mind to travel outside the country for further studies. From that moment I began to save towards this project. By this singular purpose I was able to refrain from unnecessary spending; working hard to achieve the goal of furthering my education. This did not come to reality until April 2003, when the opportunity to travel came. But before this opportunity came, investment in stock was very common. I had wanted to put all the money saved into buying shares so I could make more money and my travelling could be well funded when ready.

Reader, it is important to have your goals prioritized. And the most important one receive attention first. Travelling for further education was paramount to me, so I jettison buying shares in stocks. Even when friends' keep mentioning the financial reward of buying shares in my ears every day, I refuse to succumb to their wish; rather I was focused on my plan to further my education. By the grace of God today, I hold a PhD degree that has opened up a lot of opportunities to me. This achievement thus opens my eyes to a lot of things which I wouldn't have known or have access to if I did not make this journey. However, something happen shortly after I travelled. The stock market went into a session of turbulence, and everyone was lamenting their investment that has gone down the drain. I would have taken a portion of this predicament, but by divine providence I escaped this sudden catastrophe.

What am I saying here? Being focused and self-disciplined will take you out of a lot of life problems. Self-discipline is a necessary skill for financial success. It is an incredibly important part of personal development. The great Jim Rohn said, "We suffer from one of two things: the pain of discipline or the pain of regret." Make sure you start suffering the pain of discipline from now; because the pain of regret hurts even far more in the long run. I've got 7 tips here on how you can remain debt-free all your life if you choose to. Here they are:

Basic Steps to Debt-Free Life

Most personal finance experts are against debt, just like I am; at least to some extent. A number of them think that some debts are okay; and others belief staying out of debts is the best choice; and they may be true in some cases. For example, borrowing money to fund college education, or a graduate degree may be seen as wise decision. Of course, not every envisaged project leads to a good investment decision, and therefore, meticulous evaluation of the project before investment begins is an important step. But really, the bottom line is that outside of certain needful debt, most of it you should try to avoid if possible.

1. **Be able to distinguish between what you want, and what you truly need – and then, act accordingly**. It's great to pursue our dreams and have the life we want. The thing is, if we do so using other people's money, it can really come back to get at us later. Best to be able to first take care of what you need, and then consider what we don't need but really want.

2. **Build an emergency fund.** Keeping a fund can ensure that you are covered during times of financial distress. This could include job loss, illness, disasters, or some other calamity. These things do happen, we just don't know when and how they will take place.

3. **Spend less than you make.** This one should be common sense, though realistically everybody has a different life situation. What might be simple and no-worry for many people might be incredibly challenging for others due to their current circumstances. Regardless, we should strive to increase the gap between income and expenses.

4. **Pay off credit cards on time.** The idea of carrying credit card balances just seems so normal to so many people. I think that unless it's absolutely unavoidable, and basic needs can't be met

due to financial distress; please try to avoid carrying credit card balances.

5. **Control your emotions when shopping.** Some people just let emotions get the best of them when shopping. Having self-discipline can be a great initiative not only for finances, but for other aspects of life as well. Logic can be a great antidote for excess emotion when shopping, and an essential part of financial success.

6. **Conduct Appraisal on your spending periodically.**

   From time to time do assessment of your spending. This might be on monthly basis or bi-monthly. It implies checking your last month expenses and matching it with your set budget for that month. If your expenses are more than what you earmark in the budget for that month, it means you overspent and you need to check it.

7. **Be thankful.** Yes, there is often much to be thankful for. Even though we often see others with more money or material items, there are others who have a lot less.

An example of self-discipline and making the right choices each day was exhibited by a friend of mine, who was once out of shape. A few years back, he was definitely overweight. At that time, he was a typical example of someone who lacked self-discipline on what he consumes and did not make the right choice on his daily routine. After several failing health challenges, he decided to get fit. First he went to the gym religiously, and then added nutrition as a passion later. He started making the right choices almost every day, working out 6 days per week and truly watching what he ate. He studies nutrition to the point of it being practically a hobby of his, and actually applies this knowledge by making smart choices each passing day.

Years later, the result of his commitment and self-discipline towards putting his body in shape paid off. This guy is now in absolutely exceptional shape. He made the right choices by being disciplined, and is now enjoying a very active and healthy life. While others have shown some decline over the years, he's now clearly at a high level of fitness, well differentiated when compared to others.

I think his example can be applied to finances. If one take that approach by being self-disciplined with spending and other personal finance choices, perhaps the same success definitely will be achieved. However, you must note that there are forces against self-discipline in you that will always be working against every step of discipline you take. The human body generally, does not want anything that will take it out of its comfort zone. You need extra energy to get your body to comply with your mind's decision. I have outlined some of the tricks your body uses to get you to reject self-discipline when you choose to and what you can do.

Tricks of Forces against Self-Discipline

1. **A part of you does not want self-discipline.**

   Deep inside of you, there is a portion that wants to be completely lazy. Anytime you try to do something worthwhile, that person inside you tries everything possible to get you to stop. The only way to achieve success at learning self-discipline is to have the ability to communicate with this person inside you effectively. I'll warn you though, this person is extremely persuasive. And it's important that you realize this from the beginning. You're not going to win every battle with this person. You simply need to strive to do your best. What kind of things does this person inside of you like to say in order to make you change your mind?

2. **Five things this person says to trick you to change your mind.**

Here are the five common things that this person inside you will suggest to get you to stop doing your self-discipline resolves.

- What's the essence of this?
- Why bother? You tried it before, are you satisfied with the result?
- I'm not good enough. I don't have what it takes to get it done.
- Let's go do something else. Let's just watch some TV for a little bit.
- I'll do it later. No need to get started right now.

Reading over this list, you can see that you've said some of these things a million times to yourself. This is the little person inside you speaking. Remember, this person doesn't want you to have self-discipline; and discovered that by saying these things, it often times gets you to stop what you're doing! The trick is to realize these thoughts when they come. And kindly tell yourself that they are simply a trick to try to get you to do something else! How can you fight these tricks?

3. A great tip to get you up and going anytime, any day.

Here are some tips that will get you off the couch and start working. If for instance you want to stop watching TV and start doing school assignment, repeat to yourself, "I am doing my school assignment now. I am doing my school assignment now. I am doing my school assignment now". Take step toward what you are confessing, and see if it works or not. You'll be amazed!

4. Reject an "all or nothing" attitude in any of your commitment.

The reason we don't get started on many important things, and the reason our self-discipline weakens is because of our instinct of "all or nothing." When you start on something, start with the attitude that you are going to do your best and finish whatever you have set as goals to accomplish. When you do this, you will find yourself getting started much more quickly. And ultimately, getting a whole lot more done. Overcome any weakness on your way.

5. Ask yourself, "What is the worst that can happen?"

Fear is a spirit that inject "I can't" syndrome into you. Once it succeeds in doing this; you will always think of the negative part of the things you plan to do. How that it will not succeed or that it is impossible to do it. The best way to deal with fear is to echo "what is the worst that can happen"; this saying is the best antidote I've ever used and it's working for me. Next time you're afraid to make that phone call that you really need to make, ask yourself, "What is the worst thing that could happen?" You will be amazed by how many times the answer to this question rings "nothing". Think about the worst thing that can happen. Accept it. And then go ahead to do what you want to do.

Self-Discipline a Vital Skill in the Pursuit of Success

Self-discipline is not a trait but a skill that is much to be desired after if you choose to succeed in life. It is a skill that you need to constantly use in order to get better on whatever you are doing. It is a skill that gets better with practice. That means that if you can just begin applying it in one area of your life, soon what you learn will transfer to other areas of your life. When you are able to apply discipline to any area of your life the results will dramatically improve. Practice it every day. Because the day you stop practicing is the day you start to lose it. With this skill you are bound to achieve what many could not achieve in life. Men of reference and character we see in our societies today are people who embrace self-discipline with open arms.

Financially, self-discipline is about controlling your spending and making sure you pay for the things that need to be paid for and wasteful things are kept away from your list. The hardest part for most people is controlling their spending. If you cannot control your spending then no matter how much money you make it will never be enough. Your wants will always use up whatever income you acquire. Thus, controlling spending is a necessity for everyone. It is being able to say NO to purchases you normally make on an impulse. These impulse purchases are the primary contributors to people not following their budget. You can make a budgetary amount to account for impulse purchases but then make sure you do not go over that amount on a monthly basis.

Those who do not have a natural amount of self-discipline must acquire it the hard way. Acquiring it comes from learning to practice it in small amounts. Start by simply trying to follow your budget. Once you can do this then the next step is to be able to save money. Saving money requires you say NO to yourself when you have the urge to spend money. We often think we "must have" when in truth there is no urgency for it.

10

Financial Stability

Your plan is only helpful if you follow it. Achieving financial stability rests predominantly on setting up a budget for yourself and sticking to your budget. It is important to continually monitor your spending, savings, and investments and adjust your plan as necessary. Tracking your expenses on an ongoing basis will help you to see when you should stop spending because you have reached your limit in a particular aspect of your budget. You can use accounting software or a computer spreadsheet to track your expenses. There are also some computer budget programs that automatically track and categorize your debit and credit card purchases. If you overspend one month, try not to get discouraged. No one is perfect. If it happens often, you may need to readjust your plan so that it is more practical. For example, perhaps you can't keep your food costs at $200 a month, but you can cut back on your clothing purchases. I have outlined ten steps you can follow to launch yourself in the pathway to financial stability.

a. **Accountability**

Main thing in keeping a buoyant financial life is to be answerable to every of your financial actions. The truth is that accountability always helps to break bad habits and accumulate new ones. The biggest problem for many people is random or impulse spending. Impulse spending on eating out, shopping and online purchases is a big drain on your finances; it is the biggest budget breaker for many, and a sure way to be in dire financial tension. If you think you cannot hold yourself accountable; then secure the help of a financial advisor. One of the most beneficial aspects of having a financial advisor is the fact that you are in some manner accountable to them. The simple human desire to appear competent to someone else is often enough reason to restrict your spending when you know you'll meet with your financial advisor to go over your portfolio. However, a financial advisor is not the only way to be accountable. A spouse or a friend can serve the same purpose.

b. Continuous Knowledge and Skill Development

Your skills, knowledge and experience are the biggest asset you have. The value of your future earnings will depend on them. Your job and future career is the most important factor in achieving financial independence and security. Improving on these three assets opens the door of opportunities to you. Invest in skills and knowledge acquisition from time to time. The skill and knowledge you have today if not improved upon will become outdated tomorrow. I made a strong decision sometime back on knowledge acquisition that brought a huge door of opportunities to me today.

c. Seek Investment Opportunities

Investment opportunities will help you to establish a strong financial base for your future. However, this must be with caution because not all investment is good. Observe the business climate of such opportunity before committing yourself. My resolve not to invest in stocks sometime back cleared me from the trouble that came later. An investment on landed properties for instance, is a good decision. Land appreciates continuously. The growth of your investments over time will be amazing if you start early. Do a little research, but whatever you do, start now!

d. Cultivate the Habit of Saving

Nothing beats having a bank account that you can turn to when life gets a bit hard. Making sure that you always have money stored away will definitely give you some peace of mind. Another way to do this is to have a time deposit account. Saving is easier if you make it an automatic process. If you have direct deposit through work, you should be able to have a portion of your paycheck deposited into your savings account. Additionally, many financial institutions allow you to set up a periodic automatic transfer of funds from your checking account to your savings account. Start by simply trying to follow your budget. Once you can do this then the next step is to be able to save money. Saving money requires you say no to yourself when you have the urge to spend it.

e. Become Financially Literate

Making money is one thing; saving it and making it grow is another. Financial management and investing are lifelong endeavors. Making sound financial and investment decisions is important in achieving your financial goals. The more knowledgeable and experienced you are in financial matters, the fewer mistakes you will make. Research has shown that people who are financially literate end up with more wealth than those who are not. There is a strong monetary incentive for becoming financially sophisticated. Taking the time and effort to become knowledgeable in the areas of personal finance and investment will pay off throughout your life.

f. Take Calculated Risks

Taking calculated risks can be a prudent decision in the long run. You might make mistakes along the way, but remember, mistakes are the lessons of wisdom. Also, when you are young, you can recover faster from financial mistakes, and you have many years to recover. You often learn more from your mistakes than from your successes. Taking calculated risks when you can afford to do so is necessary to get ahead financially. Playing it safe might be a bigger mistake in the long run.

g. Cut your Spending According to your Size

This one should be common sense anyway; you know what you earn, so let your income guide you on what kind of lifestyle you should live. For instance your salary dictates that your spending should be among the middle class; but rather you are copying a friend whose spending is among the top class. For sure, you will soon be in financial tight corner. What might be a simple, no-worry matter for many people might be incredibly challenging for others due to their current circumstances. So be guided by your spending lifestyle.

h. Eliminate and Avoid Debt

It is a popular saying that the borrower is a servant to the lender. Some individuals are so comfortable with debts that they keep borrowing at every opportunity. Most of these individuals are the ones that buy thing on impulse. They have no budget, and there are no investment plans for the future. Credit card is seen today as an evil tool of wealth destruction because of impulse buying. If you've got credit cards, personal loans, or other such debt, you need to start a debt elimination plan now. List out your debts and arrange them in order from smallest balance at the top to the largest at the bottom. Then focus on the debt at the top, putting as much effort as you can into eliminating them. This could take several years, but it's a very rewarding process, and very necessary.

i. **Be a Planner**

Research has shown that those who plan for the future end up with more wealth than those who do not. Successful people are goal oriented: they set goals and develop a plan to achieve them. For example, if you set a goal to pay off your student loans in two years, you'll have a better chance of achieving this goal than you would if you merely said you wanted to pay off your student loans, but failed to set a timetable. Become a planner. Set goals and develop an action plan to reach them. Even the process of writing down some goals will help you to achieve them. Being goal oriented and following a plan means taking control of your life. It is an important step toward improving your financial independence and security.

j. Conduct Appraisal of your Set Goals Periodically

From time to time conduct occasional appraisal of set financial goals to see what have been achieved and what is remaining. This is a very clear way of knowing what you have been able to achieve and what to be improved upon.

On a final note be positive about life, and more importantly your future. You present circumstance is not a determinant of your tomorrow. But what you do with the opportunities that come your way today, determines the gains you receive tomorrow. Change the way you think; have the entrepreneur mentality. Don't confess success and always think poverty. The thought you allow in your mind is what germinates into character you exhibit; and the character you continually exhibit becomes your lifestyle. If you have not performed well in your finances in the past, at least be thankful that you have access to this financial toolkit. It will definitely make a huge impact on your destiny.

About the Author

Victor Peters is a motivational speaker and an ardent practitioner of self-improvement techniques with many years of experience in human capacity building and personal development. He has conducted training to organizations and individuals on personal development and self-improvement. After many years of studying, practicing and gaining practical experience, he decided to share the knowledge and experience he has gained, through his blog, and frequent writings in journals and other book publishing media.

Victor holds a Bachelor of Science (BSc) degree in Computer Science from the University of Wollongong Australia, a Master of Science (MSc) and Doctor of Philosophy (PhD) degree, also in Computer Science from Universiti Malaysia Sarawak (UNIMAS).

Victor Peters is the author of several books, among which are 'Find and Never Lose It', 'Is this Luck or Deliberate Working?', 'Financial Success Tool Kit', Financial Worries? Try This! Power of Thought and Action on your Mind; Financial Wisdom in the Days of Small Beginning; and 'How Best to Tame the Vindictive Monster called Poverty'.